Spell with Zip

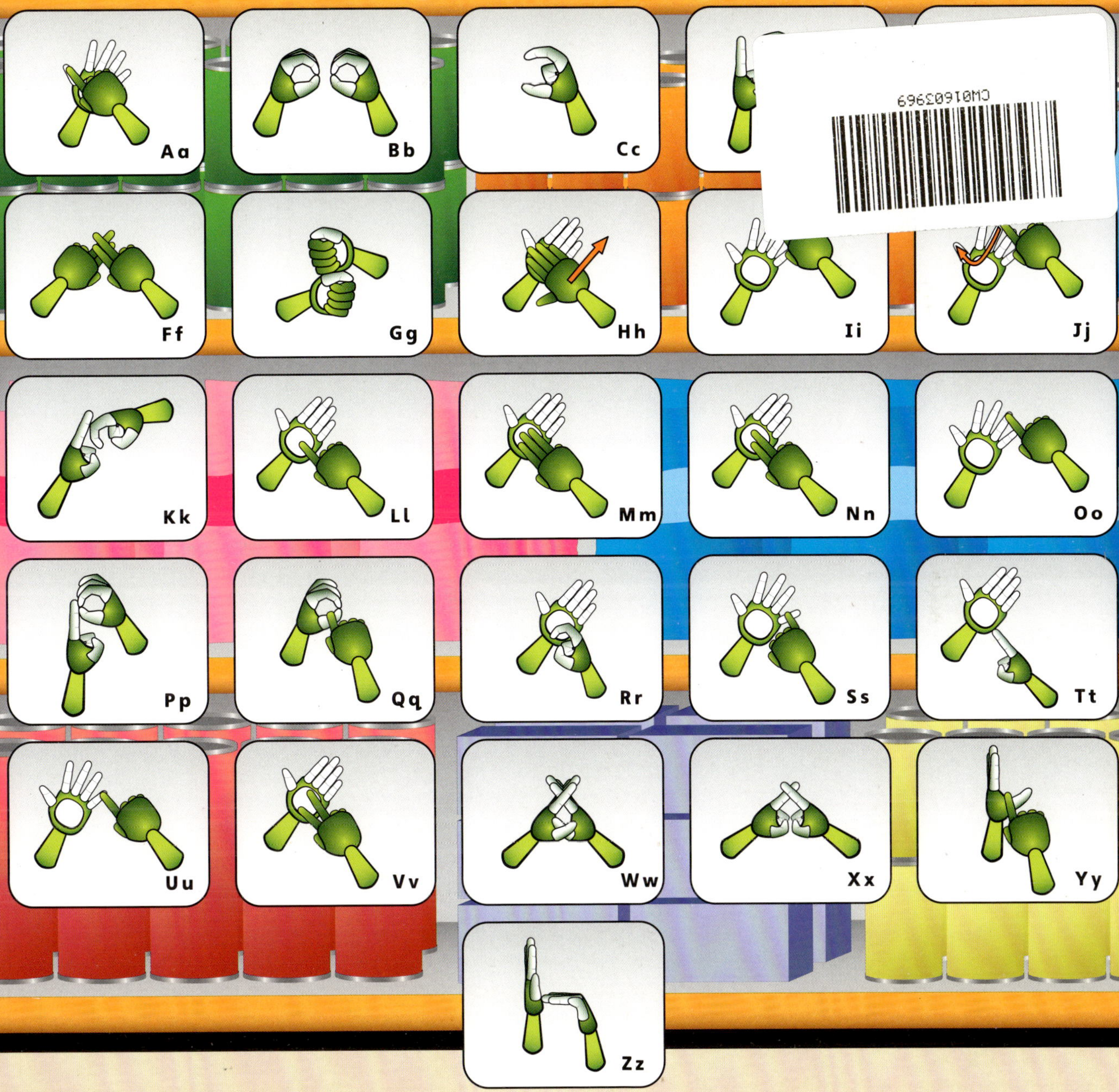

Zip

Zip is a friendly space alien from planet Zee. He loves to learn. Zip uses his hands to speak to his friends. He can't wait to teach the people of planet Earth all about sign language. Zip is the captain of his spaceship.

Pella

Pella is Zip's best friend. She also comes from planet Zee. Pella is very brave. Although she is a little younger than Zip and Statz, she isn't afraid of anything and is always the first of the three friends to try new things.

Statz

Statz is in charge of computers on the spaceship. He loves gadgets. Statz uses his Zablet to help him and his friends out of sticky situations. He is excited to learn about planet Earth and all the people who live here.

Goober

Goober is an unexpected guest on the friends' adventures. A greedy and naughty space stowaway, Goober has the ability to change his colour and shape so is always jumping out and surprising Zip, Pella and Statz.

Zip's top tips

Zip and friends are here to help you talk in a fun new way - spell with your fingers and talk with your hands. Follow these top tips to get the most from their adventures:

- **Share the book together and enjoy the story**
- **Play with the signs**
- **Use Zip's alphabet to make your own words**
- **Visit Space School, enjoy the activities and have fun**
- **Watch out for Goober...**

SignSpell

Zip at the Supermarket

The spaceship has landed early for today's adventure. Zip, Pella and Statz are in the control room getting ready.

Zip leaves his friends and heads for his morning shower.

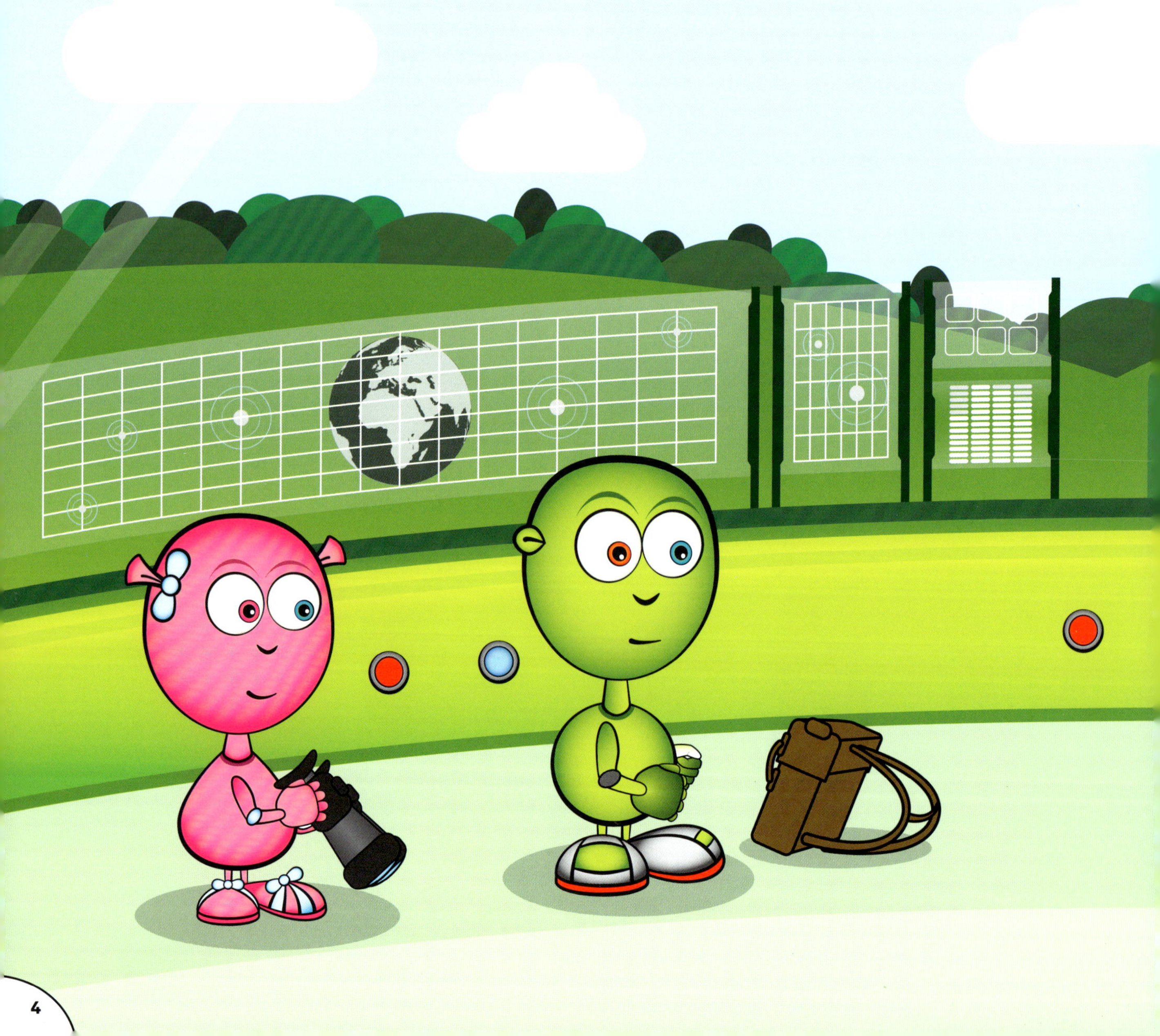

Zip turns on the shower and jumps straight in. He reaches for his shower gel and squeezes hard, but nothing comes out. The shampoo bottle is empty too.

“Ooh!” shouts Zip, “the water has turned ice cold.” He leaps from the shower and dries himself.

Shower Gel

Zip joins Pella and Statz in the kitchen. The friends need to make sure their stomachs are full for the day ahead.

“I need a nice warm drink after my cold shower,” says Zip.

Statz reaches for the hot chocolate but there is only one scoop left and Zip likes two scoops in his drink.

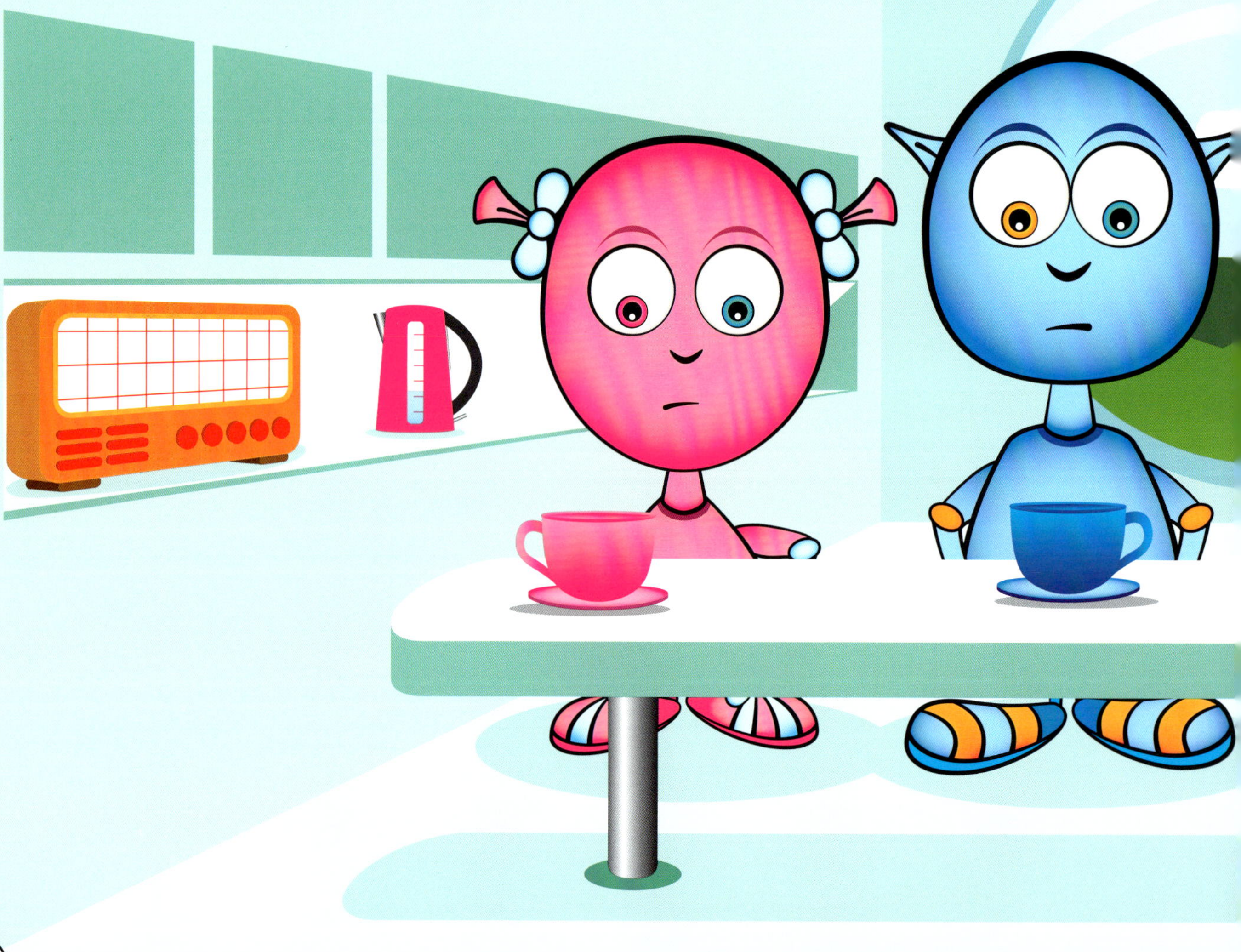

One
Two

Zip takes out the last three crumpets from the cupboard and puts them in the toaster.

“Watch out, Zip!” shouts Statz, “there’s smoke coming out of the toaster!”

Statz sprays the fire extinguisher on the toaster and covers the crumpets in foam.

Three
Foam

Zip wipes the foam off the crumpets.
"I don't think we can eat these," he says.
"Is there anything else we can eat for breakfast?"

"You can have the last of my cereal," says Pella.

Zip puts a big spoonful in his mouth.
"Yuck!" he says, spitting them back out,
"the milk tastes bad."

The friends decide to change their adventure plans.

"We need to buy some more food," says Pella.
"Today's adventure will have to be at the supermarket."

Statz takes out his Zablet. "There are four supermarkets nearby.
It will only take us five minutes to get to the nearest store."

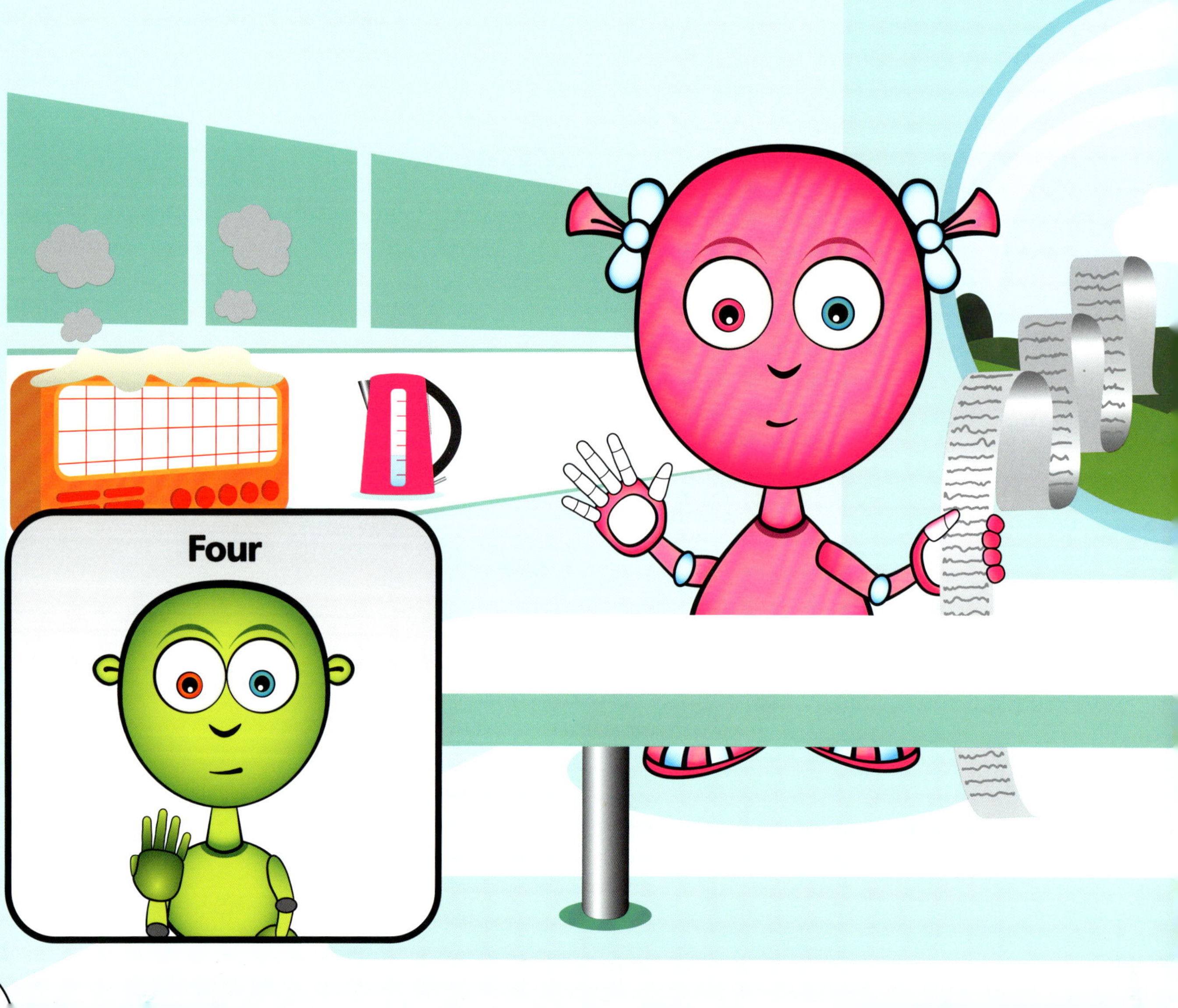

Earth Map
09:16
Supermarket
5 MINUTES FROM YOUR CURRENT LOCATION
GET DIRECTIONS>>>
CURRENT LOCATION
Five

Space School

Can you count how many fingers Zip is holding up?
See if you can spell the number using Zip's alphabet.

Zip, Pella and Statz cannot believe how big the supermarket is. "I've never seen so much food!" says Zip.

The friends grab a trolley and start ticking items off the list.

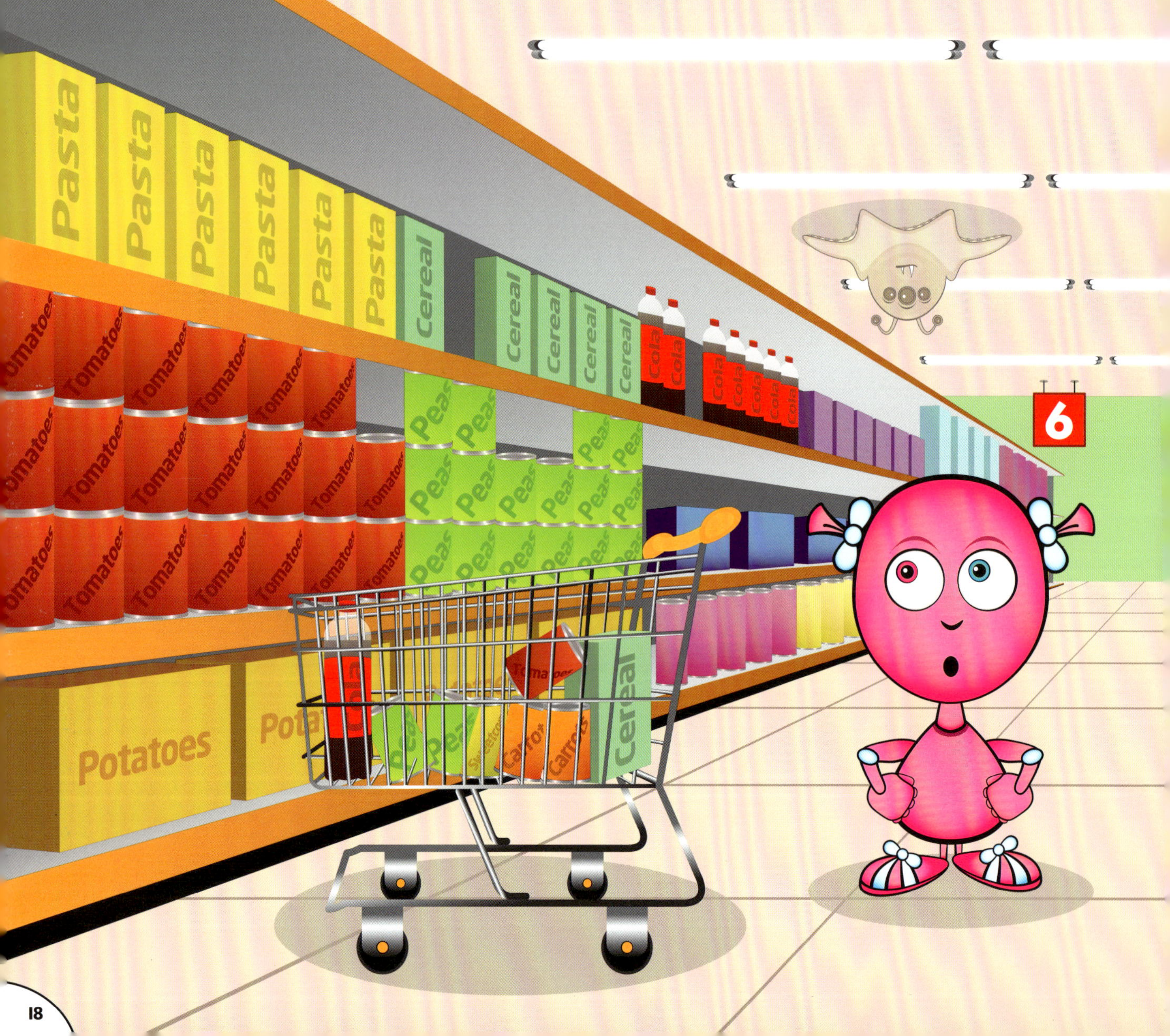

The friends go from aisle to aisle filling their trolley with lots of delicious food. By the time they reach aisle six their trolley is nearly full.

"We'd better find another trolley," says Statz.

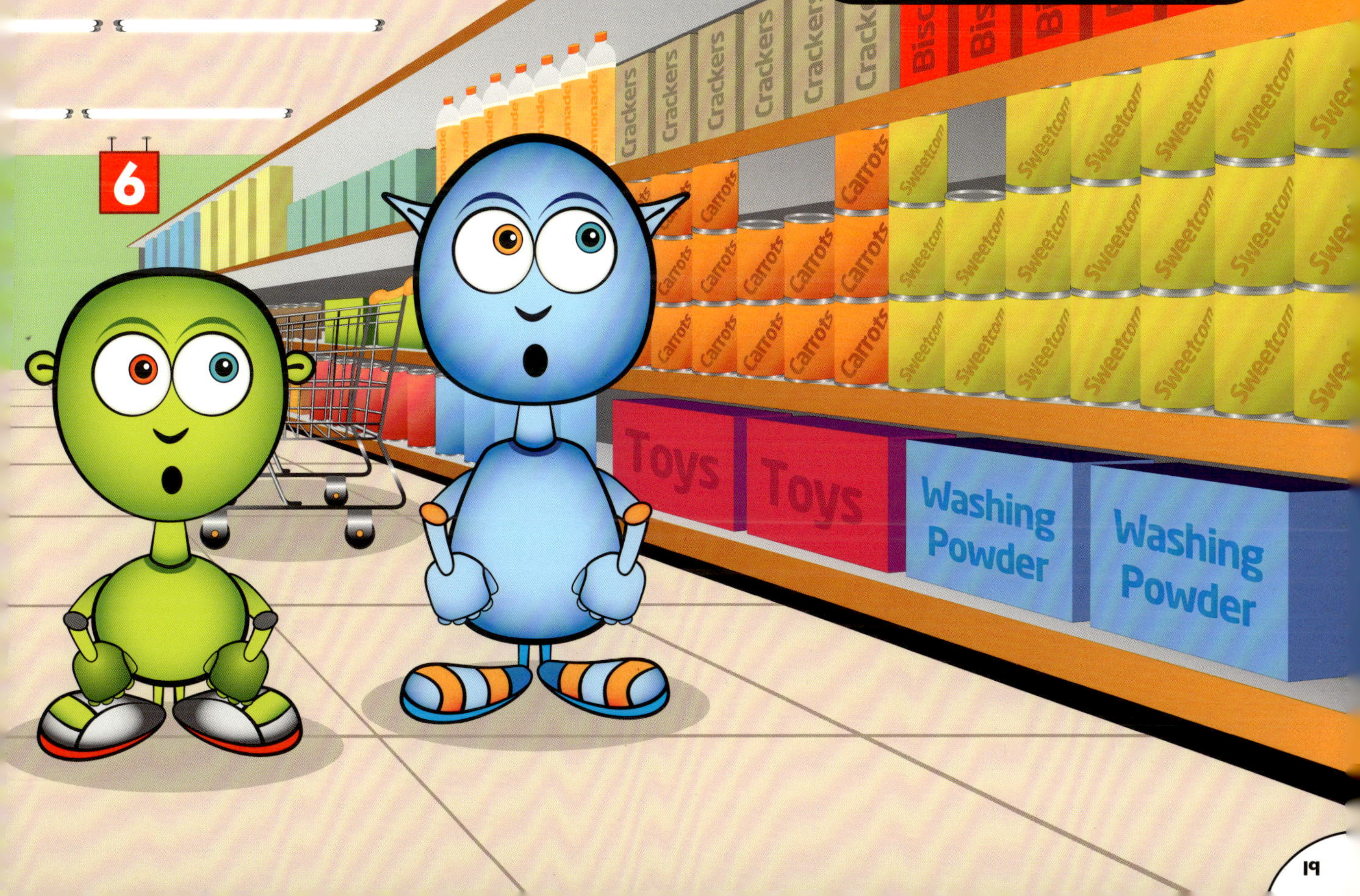

On aisle seven there is a big tower of shiny tins filled with baked beans. "I want to try those!" says Pella.

The friends all take a tin from the bottom. The shiny tins of baked beans come crashing down all around them. The tins spill all over the floor.

The friends are nearly at the end of their shopping adventure.

“Look at all those jars of sweets,” says Statz, “one jar would take me about eight days to eat.”

“More like nine minutes!” says Pella.

"Look," says Zip, "they have jars of flying saucers on the top shelf!"

The friends can't reach the shelf on their own.
"I've got an idea," says Statz. "If we stand on each other's shoulders we'll be able to reach."

"Three jars each," says Pella. She drops each jar into the trolley.
"One... two... three... four... five... six... seven... eight... nine jars of flying saucers!"

"We should get ten jars," says Zip, "so we can share one on the walk back to the spaceship."

Space School

How many items are there in the pictures below?
Can you remember how to sign the numbers?

Cup

Crumpets

Shampoo Bottles

Flying Saucers

Baked Beans

Jars

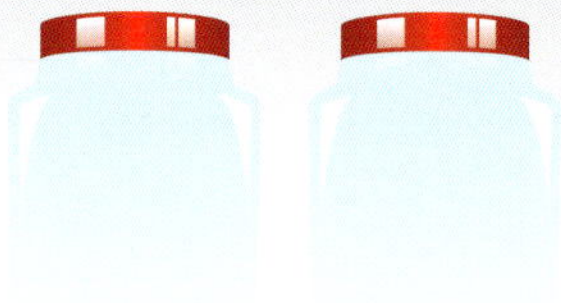

Cereal

Strawberries

Cola Bottles

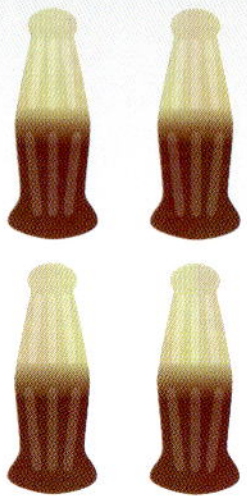

Fried Eggs

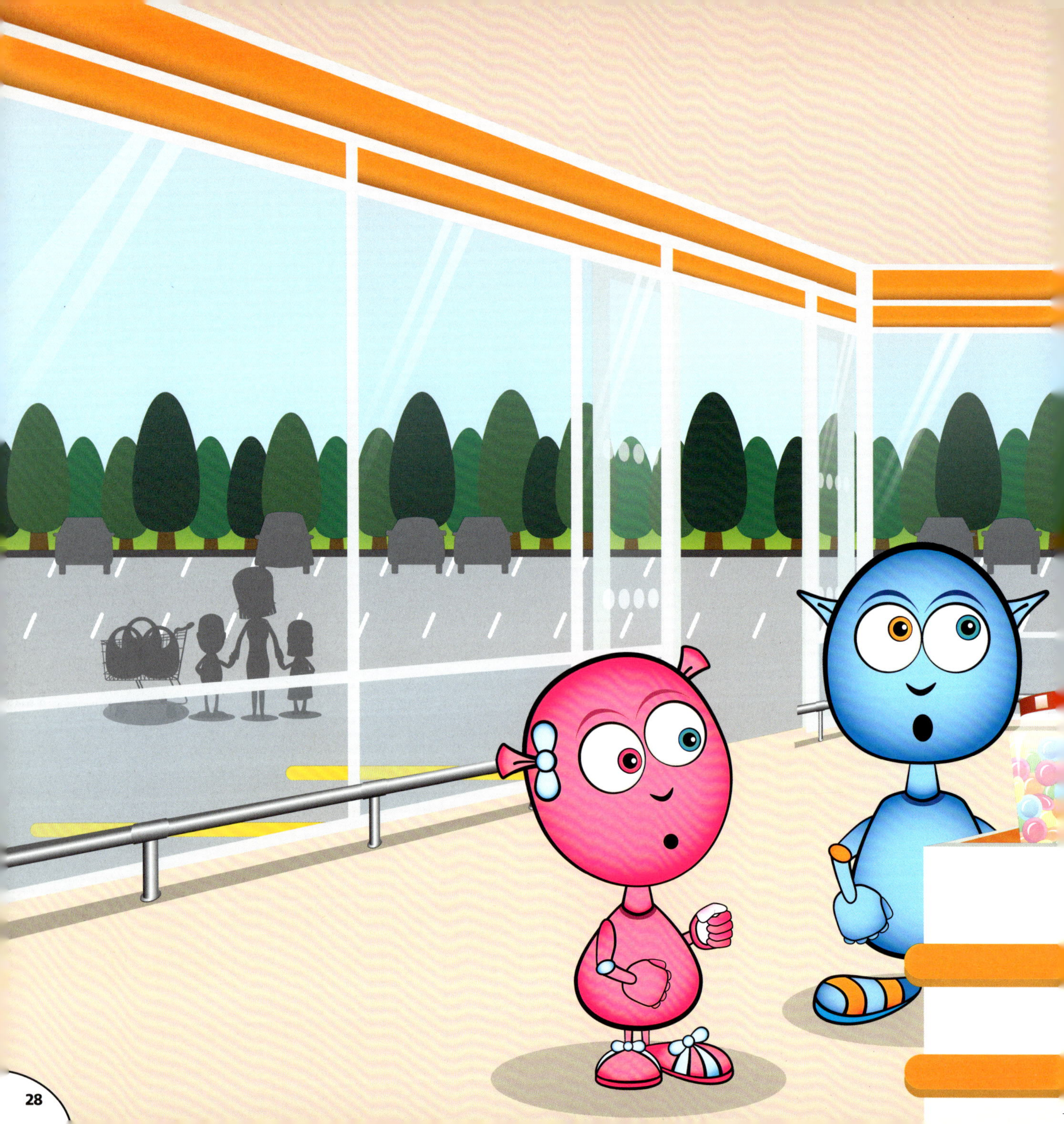

Zip, Pella and Statz have had fun at the supermarket and now they can't wait to get back to the spaceship to try all this tasty food.

They watch the human at the checkout scan each jar of sweets, one by one. She picks up the last jar but it just won't scan. She looks at the jar and starts to scream. "Aaaarrrggghhh!"

GOOBER!

Zip's Signs

Fun things to do

Now that you have read all about Zip at the Supermarket,
here are some fun things for you to do:

- **Plan a special breakfast for tomorrow morning - draw, describe or write**
- **Make up your own new sweet. What would it taste like?**
- **How would you feel if you had Zip's morning?**
- **What would you do if you knocked over a display of baked beans?**
- **How would Zip shop for food on planet Zee?**
- **Teach a friend to count to ten like Zip does**

First published 2013 by Signature

SignSpell® stories created by Signature
Designed and illustrated by Igloo Imaging Ltd.